Knowing Jesus

Pastor Jonathan Brozozog

Knowing Jesus by Pastor Jonathan Brozozog

Copyright 2021 by Jonathan Brozozog Ministries

First Printing 2021

ISBN: 978-0-9984733-1-4 (Paperback)

First Edition: 2021

Jonathan Brozozog Ministries

www.jonathanbrozozog.com

Printed in the United States of America

Table of Contents

Introduction

A Marathon, Not A Sprint

Welcome to Creative Church. But more importantly, welcome to the Christian life. I want to congratulate you on your life-changing decision to accept Jesus as your Savior and your bold determination to make him the Lord of your life.

In the Bible, the apostle Paul compared the Christian life to a race. After a lifetime of service to God, Paul was able to say, "I have fought the good fight, I have finished the race, I have kept the faith" (II Timothy 4:7, NKJV). Now the time has come for you to take your first steps in the race toward a purposeful and meaningful life. But the Christian life is not a sprint; it's a marathon. And it's a lifelong marathon whose outcome will depend on your commitment to certain spiritual fundamentals.

Any fan knows that success in a sport is determined by an athlete's commitment to the fundamentals of that sport. In golf, for instance, it's the grip. In baseball, it's catching and throwing. In football, it's running. In hockey, it's skating. But there are fundamentals in the Christian "race," as well. So in the chapters that follow, I want to introduce you to some of those fundamentals. I want to teach you the basics about communicating with God, studying God's Word, declaring your faith in an impactful way, and developing a growing relationship with the Person of the Holy Spirit.

I am also writing this book to introduce you to Creative Church, a place where Jesus is our focus and where people are our passion. Creative Church exists to help people overcome the wounds of the past so they can move steadily toward the destiny that God has in store for them.

At Creative Church, we want people to know that it's okay not to be okay. We want people to understand that there is grace for them in this place. But we also want people to know that it's not okay to stay not okay, because Jesus died for us so he could heal our invisible wounds and restore our lives. He died so he could set all of us on a course toward significance, purpose, and individual fulfillment.

At Creative Church, you will be known, loved, wanted, and appreciated. And you won't have to worry about your past mistakes, because God's grace has erased the guilt of your past, and his love has made it possible for your past failures to become the launching pad for your future success. In fact, the story of your transformation is a story we want you to learn to tell so that other people can be encouraged by your healing and restoration.

The next time you get in your car, I want you to notice how much larger your windshield is than your rear-view mirror. That's because the engineers who designed your car understood that it is more important for you to see where you are going than to see where you have been. And that is the very same lesson I want you to take from the following introduction to Creative Church and the Christian life. From God's perspective, your future is more important than your past.

Don't get me wrong! Your past was not without value. In fact, your past has great value, because God is able to take the defeats of the past and turn them into triumphs. He is able to take the sorrows of the past and turn them into wellsprings of joy. Even your biggest mistakes can become springboards to your greatest achievements if you will give God the chance to heal your wounds and teach you his eternal truths. But as you come to see with increasing clarity God's love for you and his magnificent plan for your life and as you come to realize that your greatest days are ahead of you rather than behind you, let this booklet serve as your guide through the initial steps you will take on this wonderful, lifelong journey.

You belong. You belong to the God who specializes in changing water into wine and changing broken people into people of excellence. You belong to Jesus, who placed enough value on you to take your sins upon himself and to die in your place. And you belong to God's family of believers who, though imperfect, are on their way toward the destiny that awaits them and toward the most gratifying experience that life can afford… the experience of fully knowing Jesus.

Chapter 1

Why We Pray

Let's start our journey through the basics of the Christian life with a story—a true story about a king who lived a long, long time ago.

About 700 years before the birth of Christ, the nation of Israel was divided, and the southern half of this divided nation was known as Judah. The largest city in Judah was Jerusalem, where the king of Judah lived and where he governed his people.

This king was not a perfect man by any means, but he was a better ruler than most of the kings who preceded him. He made some bad decisions that caused harm to his subjects, and at times he showed poor judgment and immaturity. The king also struggled with pride and occasional bouts of unbelief. But in spite of his periodic failures, this king of Judah worked hard to lead his people toward God instead of away from God.

But one day God sent a prophet to the king to deliver a very unsettling message. The king was sick at the time, and his health did not seem to be improving. It was during this crisis moment in the king's life that the prophet approached the king and said to him, "This is what the LORD says: Put your house in order, because you are going to die; you will not recover" (II Kings 20:1, NIV).

> **But certainly God has heard me; He has attended to the voice of my prayer.**
> **Psalm 66:19 (NKJV)**

Obviously, that was a very discouraging announcement, and it was an emphatic announcement, as well. According to the prophet, God's mind was made up, and there was no possibility that the king had misinterpreted the Lord's intentions. The prophet of God, who spoke for God and whose prophetic utterances always came true, had made it abundantly clear to the king of Judah that the king was going to die and that he needed to prepare his family for this inevitable reality. Then the prophet left the king's chambers and started to make his way back home.

But then the king did something that many people might not do under these same circumstances. The king "turned his face to the wall and prayed to the LORD... and wept bitterly" (II Kings 20:2-3, NIV).

However, as you read the biblical account through to its conclusion, notice what happened next. The Bible tells us that before the prophet "had left the middle court (of the palace), the word of the LORD came to him: 'Go back and tell (the king), the leader of my people... I have heard your prayer and seen your tears; I will heal you. On the third day from now you will go up to the temple of the LORD. I will add fifteen years to your life. And I will deliver you and this city from the hand of the king of Assyria" (II Kings 20:4-6, NIV).

Wow! Can you fully grasp what this story is saying to us today? This true story about an ancient king is telling us that prayer has the power to change God's mind. It has the power to change what God is doing in our lives. It has the power to modify God's will for those who serve him, and it has the power to turn circumstances around and to turn defeats into victories.

You see, God was absolutely clear. He didn't beat around the bush. According to God, the king was going to die. But when the king prayed, God was moved, and everything changed. Everything changed inside the king, and everything changed around the king. In fact, God went the extra mile. Not only did he heal the king; he also extended the king's life for another 15 years, and he miraculously struck down thousands of foreign soldiers who had encamped around Jerusalem in an effort to capture the city and enslave the Jewish people (read the details of this miracle in II Chronicles 32:20-21).

So prayer is the most powerful and effective tool that God has placed at the disposal of his people. Not only can prayer change the person who prays and not only can it change the circumstances surrounding that person's life, but prayer also is the most effective means at the believer's disposal for drawing near to God and for enjoying intimacy with the Lord that can result in increased faith and spiritual growth.

Nevertheless, prayer is difficult for many Christians, so a lot of God's people never really learn how to make use of this powerful tool. A lot of believers never develop a strong and consistent prayer life, which is essential to a gratifying Christian life.

How should you pray?

For starters, you should resist the temptation to make prayer more difficult than it has to be, because prayer is nothing more and nothing less than having a two-way conversation with God. That's all it is, yet that's a lot.

Just think about that for a moment. Now that you are a believer and now that you have become a child of God through faith in Jesus Christ, you get to do something that unbelievers can't do: You get to talk to God on a person-to-person and face-to-face basis, and he will meet with you when you pray. But not only will God hear you; he also has promised to respond to you and to answer you when you pray.

So the best way to talk to God is to talk to him the same way you would talk to any other person you know and trust. Think of it as an intimate conversation with somebody who loves you and cares deeply about every little thing in your life. Just say what's on your mind, and be as honest as you can be, because, like a very good friend, God already knows you through and through, so you won't need to hide your most embarrassing secrets and you won't need to filter any of your words.

> **The Lord doesn't respond to the wicked, but he's moved to answer the prayers of the righteous.**
>
> **Proverbs 15:29 (TPT)**

You also won't need to try to impress the Lord with a lot of "thee's" and "thou's" and other "religious" language, because God is not moved by lofty verbiage or fancy phrases. Only one thing impresses God: simple, straightforward, honest talk that flows from a believing heart—the same kind of honest, heartfelt talk that the king of Judah used when he turned his face to the wall and cried like a baby. After all, God already knows what you are thinking before you say it, and he already knows what you need before you tell him (see Matthew 6:32). So why would you want to waste your time trying to impress him with unnecessary gobbledygook?

Also, don't forget that you will be engaging in a conversation, not a one-way speech. So learn to listen to God as much as you talk to him. God will speak to you when you pray. He will speak to your mind through new and powerful thoughts that he places there. He will speak to your heart through memories that he summons from the past. He will speak to your soul through strong images (pictures) that he places within your consciousness. God has a lot more important things to say to you than you have to say to him, and that is why God spoke to the sons of Korah and told them, "Be still, and know that I am God" (Psalm 46:10, NKJV).

> **Prayer is a conversation with God. During prayer we need to speak but also listen. We listen to hear what God is saying in response to our petitions. You do not need to use a filter when you talk to God.**

You will never learn to pray if prayer feels like work to you. You will only learn to pray effectively when your prayers start to feel like an intimate conversation with someone who knows you perfectly and yet loves you perfectly. So prayer is not a begging session, and it's not a complaint session either, because complaining is just a way of telling God that you disagree with the way he's running your life. Prayer is simply talking to God about the deepest needs, secrets, dreams, and fears that fill the secret recesses of your heart and mind.

Sometimes, of course, you will have to tell your Heavenly Father about the things that are troubling you, and sometimes you will find it necessary to tell him about the needs you have in your life. But for the most part, prayer must always be simple "communion." Prayer is a very natural, very honest, very straightforward conversation with God about all the important things that are happening inside you and around you. It's an opportunity for you to bring to God all those things you want to leave with him and to take from God all those things he wants to leave with you. God is the only person you can totally trust with your deepest needs and struggles, because God cannot be shocked by anything and he cannot be fooled, deceived, or surprised. So learn to take advantage of the Lord's invitation to talk to him candidly and regularly.

When should you pray?

Practice doesn't make perfect; practice makes permanent. So if you want a powerful prayer life, you're going to have to work at making prayer a permanent part of your daily routine.

I would suggest that you start developing your new habit of prayer by praying constantly throughout the day whenever the need or an appropriate opportunity arises. In those situations, you don't need to kneel or even close your eyes, and you don't need to pray out loud. It's easy to develop a habit of just silently thanking God for his goodness to you or silently asking God to help a person who has confided in you regarding a challenge in his or her life. Paul told the believers in one 1st-century church to "make your life a prayer" (I Thessalonians 5:17, TPT). In other words, prayer should be something that is ongoing in your life.

> **This is the reason I urge you to boldly believe for whatever you ask for in prayer—be convinced that you have received it and it will be yours.**
>
> **Mark 11:24 (TPT)**

But in addition to these spontaneous occasions of prayer, you should also develop a more structured time to shut the door on the rest of the world and focus exclusively on God. You should develop the habit of setting aside a specific time each day to converse with the Lord. After all, that is the best way to create and maintain this new behavior in your life.

But what time is the best time to pray? Well, the Bible gives us some hints, but God doesn't specifically tell us to pray at certain times of the day. He leaves that up to us.

I recently went into a sporting goods store to buy some exercise equipment, and I asked the salesman, "Which piece of equipment would be best for helping me lose some weight?"

The salesman responded, "The one that you will use."

And that's the best way to approach prayer, as well. Pick the time of day or night that works best for you… the time that you can most consistently devote yourself to God.

> **You were created in the image and likeness of God. Spend time with God, and you will become more like Him.**

Personally, I think the best times are the first thing in the morning and the last thing at night. The Bible also suggests that these are really good times for spiritual focus (see Deuteronomy 6:7, 11:19). But there's no fixed rule here. The Christian life is all about freedom, not conformity to a bunch of religious rituals.

The reason I suggest the mornings and the evenings as the best times for prayer is because you know that you're "addicted" to a behavior when that behavior becomes the first thing you want to do each day and the last thing you want to do each night. And since the goal here is to become "addicted" to prayer rather than the unhealthy behaviors that may have imprisoned you in the past, you need to develop the habit of starting and ending each day with prayer. Besides, the way you start your day and the way you end your day will speak loudly about the way that you live your day. And the way you begin your day and conclude your day will determine the way that you prioritize your day and order your day. When you start each day and end each day in God's presence, you will find that God's presence and blessings follow you throughout the mundane and sometimes challenging episodes of your daily life.

Where should you pray?

Again, the Christian life does not consist of a series of religious rules, so there's no command in the Bible regarding the places you should pray. However, common sense and a great deal of personal experience compel me to recommend that you find your own special place to pray. Jesus prayed in lonely places apart from his disciples, Abraham prayed under the starry nighttime sky, and Adam met with God in the cool of the Garden of Eden. You, too, should find your own "cool place" to pray.

> **Let this hope burst forth within you, releasing a continual joy. Don't give up in a time of trouble, but commune with God at all times.**
>
> **Romans 12:12 (TPT)**

If possible, I would also suggest that you modify your prayer environment to make your prayer time as easy and as comfortable as possible. After all, you want to train your brain to create a new habitual behavior in your life, and the best way to teach your brain a new habit is by rewarding your brain (positive reinforcement) for engaging in this new activity.

That is why it might be a good idea to play some praise and worship music while you pray. You may also want to dim the lights or sit in your favorite chair while you pray. The idea here is to make your prayer environment as comfortable and inviting as possible so you can get your mind off other things and focus on talking to God about the things that are going on in your life. And you don't need to feel constrained to pray for any specific length of time. After all, some of the most powerful prayers in the Bible were short prayers (the king of Judah prayed and God answered his prayer before the prophet had time to leave the palace).

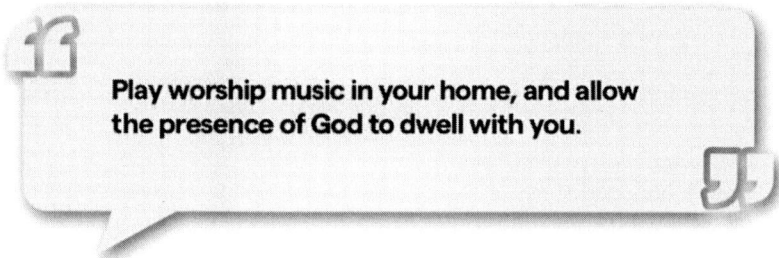

> **Play worship music in your home, and allow the presence of God to dwell with you.**

Finally, I would recommend keeping a prayer journal, which should be something like a spiritual diary. Make notes about all the things you shared with the Lord during your time with him, and cross off each item as God responds to that specific aspect of your conversations with him. You can also write down testimonies and praise reports as God moves in your life to answer particular requests. Believe me, a written record of God's faithfulness to you will build your own faith tremendously as the years pass by and as you experience the dependability of the Lord.

And never forget to be open, honest, and real. Learn to lift your hands in worship. After all, nobody will be watching you. And learn to sing your own "solo" to the Lord ("so low" that nobody else can hear you). Then learn to listen as much as you talk. Remember, it's a conversation, not a speech and not a begging session.

Planning to pray

Finally, I recommend that you develop a simple strategy for your prayer life, because you can't be a disciple without being disciplined in the important areas of your life. Your strategy doesn't have to be complicated, but you do need some sort of game plan for your time with the Lord. When you call a friend on the phone, you always have a reason for calling that person, and you know exactly what you want to say before the person answers the phone. However, many people approach their prayer time without any clear objective in mind, and this often makes their prayer time empty and meaningless as they repeat the same two or three concerns each day.

The Bible doesn't give us a specific strategy for prayer, but the Bible does tell us to pray for certain things. So, based on the directives of God's Word, here is a simple model that might help you get started. This model prayer strategy starts with you personally and then radiates outward to touch all the areas of your life that should be the constant focus of your prayers:

- **Mondays** – pray for yourself (your spiritual life, your struggles, your dreams)
- **Tuesdays** – pray for your family (your spouse, your children, your parents)
- **Wednesdays** – pray about your professional pursuits and your finances
- **Thursdays** – pray for your church and its leaders, as well as the people you know who have specific needs in their lives
- **Fridays** – pray for your country and for God's work around the world
- **Saturdays** – have a regular family prayer time (perhaps at breakfast)
- **Sundays** – pray for salvations in the day's church services and then go to church to worship, to give thanks, and to allow God to speak to your heart

Obviously, this is just a guide. Each day, you will find that the circumstances of life compel you to pray for a lot of things that are not on this list. But a prayer strategy like this one can help you broaden your prayer life so you don't get stuck praying for the same thing every day. A strategy like this one will also help you extend your prayer focus beyond yourself.

Conclusion

Like anything meaningful in life, prayer is something that must be learned. But unlike a lot of things, prayer is best learned, not by reading about it in a book or hearing about it from a sermon, but through personal effort and hands-on experience.

I am praying for your success in the Christian life and for your rapid growth in the things of God. But nothing is more important or more fundamental to your long-term success than your own strong and consistent prayer life. So learn to pray like all the men and women in the Bible prayed so that God can change those things that need to be changed in your life and do those things that need to be done in the areas of your life that matter most. Follow the advice of the apostle Paul and learn to "make your life a prayer" (I Thessalonians 5:17, TPT).

Questions for thought and discussion

1. In the preceding chapter, Pastor Jonathan wrote about the importance of listening to God at least as much as you talk to God. Can you think of an occasion when God spoke directly to you about something important in your life? What did God say? How did he communicate with you?

_____

_____

_____

_____

2. According to Pastor Jonathan, "practice doesn't make perfect; practice makes _____ (fill in the blank)." What does this observation mean to you? What does it mean for your prayer life?

_____

_____

3. In the Bible, we learn that Jesus prayed early in the morning, and he prayed late at night. We also learn that he periodically withdrew from his disciples for long sessions of prayer, and he frequently prayed before and after ministering to large groups of people. What are the best times for you to engage in prayer? Why?

_____

_____

_____

_____

4. Adam met with the Lord in the Garden of Eden during "the cool of the day" (see Genesis 3:8). What is your ideal "cool place" to pray? Does that place currently exist, or will you have to create it? Describe the kind of environment that would be most conducive to your prayer life.

_____

_____

_____

_____

Chapter 2

The Most Important Book Ever

The Bible is the most unique book ever written. For one thing, the Bible is more than one book; the Bible is a book that is composed of many different books. The Bible consists of 66 different standalone books that were written by 44 different writers over a period of about 1500 years. Most of these writers never met one another, so they did not have the luxury of collaborating while they were writing their distinctive books. In addition, most of these writers had no access to the other writers' works, so they couldn't coordinate their material or cross-check their information to construct the biblical text.

Nevertheless, after these 44 writers had died and after their works were brought together, the world learned that these 66 different books actually fit together like a brilliantly designed jigsaw puzzle. When combined, they told one seamless story, the story of God's redemptive plan for the human race. They also combined to bear witness to one God, who is always consistent with himself throughout the 66 individual books within the Bible. The 66 standalone books also merged to offer hundreds of the most unlikely predictions about the future, predictions that have never failed to prove true. And they merged to point to one great apex of human history—the death, burial, and resurrection of Jesus Christ. Everything that was written before Christ pointed forward to his death and resurrection, and everything that was written after Christ pointed backward to his death and resurrection. These 66 individual books, therefore, combined to present one way to be saved and one way for people to believe rightly about God.

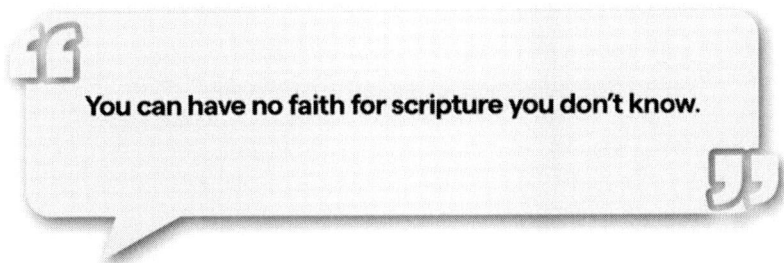

> **You can have no faith for scripture you don't know.**

So unlike any of the literary masterpieces of merely human design, the Bible is a supernatural book. It is miraculous in its origins, because, by reading the works of the 66 individual authors, the reader of the biblical text can clearly see the guiding hand and personal oversight of the Holy Spirit, who allowed these human authors to write in their own individual styles, but who simultaneously guided them so they wrote the exact words that God wanted them to write.

This means that the Bible is timeless. It speaks to all people, no matter when they might have lived in the past or where they might live today. And the Bible is relevant to you and to everybody else in 21st-century America, because God never changes, and his truths never change. Consequently, the Word of God is still the bread of life for those who want to grow in their relationship with the Lord, and the Bible is still the primary vehicle through which God speaks to those who want to know him.

Why so many versions?

As you begin to read and study the Bible, you will soon notice that the Bible is published in many different "versions." There's the New

International Version, the New English Bible, the English Standard Version, and many, many more. All of these "versions" of the Bible are taken from the same original text (the Bible was originally written in Hebrew, Aramaic, and Greek). However, translators have used a multitude of different styles to translate the original languages into modern English, and new versions are being published every year to keep pace with the changing language of modern English-speaking countries.

> **All Scripture is given by inspiration of God, and is profitable for doctrine, for reproof, for correction, for instruction in righteousness, that the man of God may be complete, thoroughly equipped for every good work.**
> **II Timothy 3:16-17 (NKJV)**

At Creative Church, we use the New King James Version (NKJV), and we would encourage you to start your Bible reading regimen with the New King James Version, as well. Why? So you can hear the same language from the pulpit that you are reading at home. Nevertheless, any good version of the Bible is acceptable if you find that you prefer a different version (The Passion Translation is also excellent). If you find a version of the Bible that speaks more clearly to you, buy it and use it daily, because you want to read the Bible for revelation, not information. You want to understand it and be able to absorb it and remember what you have read.

As you start to read, however, you will quickly discover two important facts about the Bible that will influence your ability to absorb what you have read.

- First, you will learn that the Bible is composed of many different "genres" of literature. Most of the Bible is historical narrative (true stories about real, historical people). However, the Bible also contains laws, poems, pithy sayings, sermons, letters, parables, genealogies, chronicles, riddles, drama, biographical sketches, and prophetic oracles that are filled with a lot of strange symbols and imagery. Because of this diversity in literary genres, the Bible can be challenging at times, but it should never be boring.

> **Don't read the Bible to finish it. Read the Bible to understand, get revelation, and grow.**

- The second thing you will notice is that the Bible is designed to serve as a spiritual "mirror" for the person who reads it. Because the Bible is more than a merely human book and because it flows from God himself, the Bible is the only book in the world that can read you while you are reading it. The words of the Bible will force you to see yourself more clearly than you have ever seen yourself before. It will also enable you to peer into the secret recesses of your own heart and mind so you can learn as much about yourself as you learn about God. But the Bible is designed this way to help you grow as a Christian. In fact, it is designed to be your greatest source of spiritual nourishment, because the Bible will help you identify those areas of your life that you need to surrender to God, but it will also show you the glorious blessings that await you as you submit yourself to the Lord.

Why Bible reading is important

There are three reasons that your Christian growth will depend on your willingness to read and study the Bible:

1. The Bible will speak truth to your heart and mind.

I encourage you to take your Bible with you and to read it during your prayer time, because the Bible will speak to you about your life, and the things that God shows you will help you understand how you should pray.

> But be doers of the word, and not hearers only, deceiving yourselves. For if anyone is a hearer of the word and not a doer, he is like a man observing his natural face in a mirror; for he observes himself, goes away, and immediately forgets what kind of man he was. But he who looks into the perfect law of liberty and continues in it, and is not a forgetful hearer but a doer of the work, this one will be blessed in what he does.
>
> James 1:22-25 (NKJV)

For instance, the Bible at times may speak to you about attitudes or behaviors in your life that need to be changed, and that insight may lead you to ask God's forgiveness for your mistakes along with his help to change. At other times, the Bible may speak to you about one of the promises that God has made to his children (including you), and that revelation may lead you to "declare" God's promises while you pray and to ask God to make those promises a reality in your life.

As you read the Scriptures—especially as you read the true stories of people who walked with God in times past—you will come to better understand the kinds of needs that God wants to satisfy in the believer's life and the kinds of battles that believers must face, and those insights will help guide you as you seek to deal with similar challenges in your own life.

In other words, the Bible will help you better understand how you should pray and what you should pray for, because God's will for your life is that you grow in faith and righteousness and that you become a little bit more like Jesus with each passing day. However, that kind of spiritual growth can only be achieved as you spend time with the Lord and as you talk to him on the same wavelength that he is talking to you through the Bible.

2. The Bible will build your faith.

The Christian life has a lot of "highs," so you will enjoy your Christian journey. But life itself has a lot of "lows," and you won't be able to successfully navigate those low times if you don't know what to expect from God when life throws you a curve ball.

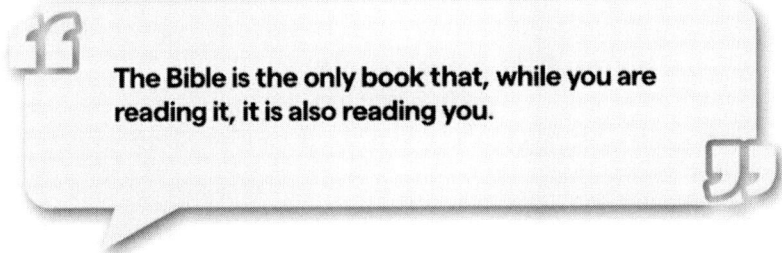

> **The Bible is the only book that, while you are reading it, it is also reading you.**

That is why God's Word is so important to your Christian growth. However, you won't be able to absorb God's wisdom by placing the Bible under your pillow at night, hoping that its information will somehow seep into your brain. You can only absorb God's wisdom and understand God's will for your life by taking the time to feed your soul on the written words that God has made available to you. As you read the Bible and come to better understand God and his ways, your faith will increase and your spirit will be strengthened.

The Bible itself tells us that "faith comes by hearing, and hearing by the word of God" (Romans 10:17, NKJV). Therefore, to build faith in your own heart, you need to hear (or read) God's Word, because you can't believe a promise of God that you have never heard, and you can't have faith in a scripture that you don't know exists.

You were recently saved. You recently gave your heart to Christ. But why did you take that bold step? You took that step because you heard a message of God's truth that spoke to you about God's love for you and your need for him, and that revelation awakened faith in your heart. You knew that it was true when you heard it, and so you acted upon it. And because you acted upon it in faith, it produced something real and eternal in your soul. It completely changed your life.

Well, there's a lot more spiritual truths waiting for you in the pages of the Bible. The Bible is filled with revelations and promises about the things that God wants to do for you. There are also untold numbers of revelations concerning the person of God himself—who he is, how he thinks, how he acts in people's lives. But you cannot know these things or believe these things until you hear these things or read these things. Yet as you read them and believe them, they will take root in your heart and produce the same kind of miraculous results that you experienced when you believed the salvation message and surrendered your life to Christ.

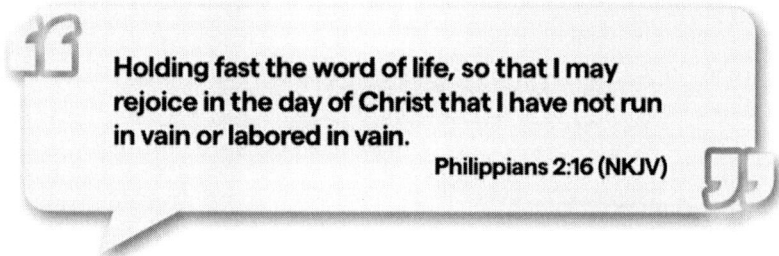

> **Holding fast the word of life, so that I may rejoice in the day of Christ that I have not run in vain or labored in vain.**
>
> **Philippians 2:16 (NKJV)**

3. The Bible will save your soul.

You are already saved, and you are destined for Heaven, because, when you believed the Gospel message and prayed the prayer of faith, your spirit was immediately saved. But your soul is another matter. The soul isn't saved instantaneously. The soul (the mind, the will, the emotions, the affections, the memories, your personality) is something that God will change gradually over the course of your life. You will never stop growing in your knowledge of Christ and your obedience to him.

So, when it comes to your eternal spirit, you cannot get "more saved." Your sins have been completely forgiven—all of them—and you are bound for Heaven. But while your spirit is saved, your mind (your soul) needs to be renewed on a daily basis (see Romans 12:2). Likewise, your emotions need to be healed and your affections need to be redirected away from worldly attractions and toward God. Your memories also need to be transformed, along with a lot of other things like your attitudes, your language, your spending habits, your parenting skills, your work ethics, etc. On the level of the soul, you need to grow a little bit every day.

But how can God make these incremental changes in your life? How can he lift you from one level of righteousness to another? How can he cause you to grow and to become everything that he has destined you to be? He will do all these things through the impact of his Word upon your life. Through his Word, he will correct you when you are wrong (see II Timothy 3:16). Through his Word, he will change the way that you think. Through his Word, he will place the perfect image of Christ before you every day and then, by the power of the Holy Spirit, will gradually change you from one degree of spiritual maturity to the next until you eventually think and act like Jesus in every dimension of your life.

God changed your heart so he could change your mind (see Romans 12:2). If God had started with your mind, your sinful nature would have resisted him. But God started with your heart, and he changed your heart in a moment of time. And now he has access to your mind, which he will change gradually throughout the course of your life. Through his written Word, God will show you what you need to know about yourself and he will show you what you need to know about him and about living the Christian life in a sinful world. The Bible will help you develop new priorities, new attitudes, and new perspectives on every aspect of your earthly life as you learn to think differently about them. But you can only learn what God has for you if you take the time to read God's words to you. You can only saturate your thinking with God's truths if you take the time to "bathe" your mind in his Word.

> So then faith comes by hearing, and hearing by the word of God.
>
> Romans 10:17 (NKJV)

Conclusion.

There are some things about God that we can understand without the Bible. For instance, we don't need to read the Bible to know that God exists, because God himself has told us that his creation (his handiwork) proves his existence (see Romans 1:20). Likewise, we don't need the Bible to understand some of the basic attributes of God's personality. God's creation bears witness to his kindness and his love (see Acts 14:17).

But we do need to read or hear the message of the Bible in order to be saved. We also need to read the Bible to clearly understand God's nature and his ways, because left to our own imaginations, we humans are too easily inclined to create our own erroneous ideas about God. And finally, we need the Bible to comprehend God's perfect will for our lives—what is right in his eyes, what is wrong, and how he wants us to behave in the presence of certain challenges and opportunities.

So start reading and studying your Bible as soon as possible. You may not understand everything you read at first. You may even be offended by some of the things you read. But by picking up the Bible and feeding your soul upon its powerful truths, you will be laying the foundation for a strong and fruitful life that is marked with God's blessings and favor.

Questions for thought and discussion

1. According to Pastor Jonathan, "The Bible is the only book in the world that can read _____ while you are reading _____" (fill in the blanks). What does this statement mean?

Have you found this to be true while reading the Bible for yourself? Explain!

_____

_____

_____

_____

2. We learn in Chapter 2 that the Bible speaks truth to the believer's heart and mind. Do you have a personal story to tell about the way God has spoken directly to your heart or mind through his written Word?

_____

_____

_____

_____

3. One of the primary reasons God has preserved his words for us in written form is to provide us with a source of truth that can build our faith. Describe a situation where the Word of God gave you faith to believe the Lord and to trust him in a difficult situation.

_____

_____

_____

_____

4. In Chapter 2 you learned that "God changed your _____ so he could change your _____" (fill in the blanks). Describe a real-life situation where the Holy Spirit has used the words of the Bible to change your thinking or your attitude about something important.

Chapter 3

The Wedding Ring Of Christianity

Were you baptized when you were a child? Perhaps you were baptized when you were so young that you don't even remember the experience. In many traditional churches, it is common to baptize children or even infants, but here at Creative Church we "dedicate" infants and small children while we baptize adults and children who are old enough to understand the significance of what they are doing.

You see, water baptism is more than a mere ritual. It is more than a religious ceremony. Throughout history, baptism has been a really big deal for God's people, because the choice to participate in water baptism shows that the participant has made a life-changing decision for Christ and has crossed a line that will not allow him to return to his former, sinful life. To the individual who participates in baptism and to the society that witnesses it, water baptism is truly a watershed moment. In other words, it is an event that marks a unique and important change of course in an individual's life.

When Jesus was 40 days old, Joseph and Mary fulfilled their spiritual responsibility as parents by dedicating him to the Lord (see Luke 2:22-24). But when Jesus turned 30 years old, he took it upon himself to be baptized (see Matthew 3:13). A person can only be legitimately baptized when that person is old enough and mature enough to understand the true meaning of what he or she is doing, because water baptism is an outward expression of an inward experience. If a person has not had the inward experience of being born again, that person should not participate in baptism, because it will be nothing more to him than a meaningless ritual. But if a person has had a genuine salvation experience, baptism is both acceptable to God and essential to the growth of that new believer.

In the New Testament church, baptism was not optional. At the command of Jesus, the apostles preached the Gospel throughout the known world, and then they baptized every person who made a confession of faith in response to their preaching (see Matthew 28:10). Baptism is the logical and biblical "next step" for the person who commits to Christ.

> **Baptism is an outward expression of an inward change. In baptism we identify with Christ's death, burial, and resurrection.**

A present-day analogy

A good way to understand what baptism meant to Jesus and to the writers of the New Testament is to look at the illustration of the modern-day wedding ring. Water baptism is the "wedding ring" of Christianity.

A wedding ring doesn't make you married any more than water makes you saved. Any woman can buy a wedding ring and place it on her finger, but that ring doesn't mean anything unless a real experience (marriage) is attached to it. The same is true when it comes to water baptism. Any person can be baptized—any adult, any child, any infant—but unless that person's baptism is attached to a life-changing encounter with Christ, the act of baptism will prove to be nothing more than an opportunity to get wet. When baptism assumes its rightful place as an outward expression of an inward experience, the experience of water baptism can be a deeply meaningful and intensely memorable experience, just like the exchange of rings at a wedding ceremony can be meaningful and memorable. In fact, who would want to get married without exchanging rings?

> There is also an antitype which now saves us—baptism (not the removal of the filth of the flesh, but the answer of a good conscience toward God), through the resurrection of Jesus Christ.
>
> I Peter 3:21 (NKJV)

Water baptism, like a wedding ring, also makes people aware that you have dedicated your life to another. By wearing a wedding ring, you put the whole world on notice that your heart belongs to someone else. And by submitting yourself for water baptism, you make all those who witness your baptism aware that you have truly devoted your heart to Christ.

Flirting is the language of the unclaimed. When you engage in flirting—even innocent flirting—you are making the world around you aware that your heart belongs to nobody. You are uncommitted as far as marriage and romance are concerned. But when you finally find the right person and you enter into a relationship, you no longer flirt with other people. And so it is with the believer! The person who has surrendered his or her heart to the Lord is a person who no longer "flirts" with the world, with sin, or with the person he or she used to be. Through baptism, therefore, the new believer is making a public declaration that he (or she) has yielded his heart to Christ, and he is declaring that he wants the world to know about his change of course. He is unashamed and unapologetic about the God he has chosen to serve, the same way that a new bride is unashamed and unapologetic about the man she has chosen to marry.

> Baptism demonstrates our commitment to a relationship with Christ. When your life is transformed, like someone who just got engaged, you want everyone to know about it. Flirting is the language of the uncommitted.

When it is done for the right reasons, water baptism can be a supernatural and life-changing experience, not because there is special power in the water or in the words that the minister might say. The experience can be powerful and life changing because God honors obedience and he honors faith. Through baptism a person expresses his faith that Jesus died for him. Through baptism a person also expresses his obedience to the Lord, who commanded us to be baptized. That's why many times I have watched people come up out of the water healed and delivered. I have seen people suddenly attain a new sense of God's presence or personal freedom from a powerful addiction. I have seen people instantly delivered from envy, guilt, and a host of other imprisoning emotions. Preceded by a genuine encounter with Christ, water baptism can be a powerful and impactful experience. But apart from a personal salvation experience, it can be quite hollow.

> But when they believed Philip as he preached the things concerning the kingdom of God and the name of Jesus Christ, both men and women were baptized.
>
> **Acts 8:12 (NKJV)**

The significance of baptism

The ordinance of water baptism is significant in at least three ways:

1. Baptism is an outward expression of an inward experience.

If you have been saved, then, through your faith in Jesus Christ, you enjoy the peace of being forgiven by God and the joy of being accepted by the Lord as his child. Your "old man" has been crucified with Christ, and your "new man" is already being created through the work of the Holy Spirit in your heart. So baptism is a "picture" of these events. By participating in baptism, you show that your old nature has died and that the "old you" has been buried (under the water). You also show that you have been raised to new life (by being raised up out of the water).

2. Baptism is the public profession of your faith and salvation.

If you have invited Christ into your life, you are a new person. However, that was a personal experience between you and God. The act of water baptism declares your salvation to the whole world. As stated above, it is the "wedding ring" that showcases your newfound devotion to the Lord, and it points to the one who is the new focus of all your affections, Jesus Christ.

> **Baptisms can be scheduled on the church's website at creativechurch.com**

3. Baptism is an act of worship.

The Bible teaches us that obedience is an act of worship (see I John 5:3). And since Jesus commanded all believers to be baptized after they were saved, submission to this command becomes an act of willful obedience to the Lord. Therefore, it becomes a significant form of worship.

The proper mode of baptism

The New Testament speaks often about the subject of water baptism, but only one passage of scripture gives us significant insight into the proper mode of baptism for the person who accepts Christ as Savior. In Acts 8, the Holy Spirit instructed Philip, a prominent leader in the early church, to share the gospel with a foreign dignitary who was reading the book of Isaiah while traveling from Jerusalem back to his home in Ethiopia.

After Philip had shared the gospel with this Ethiopian, the man accepted Christ, and, noticing a nearby body of water, suggested to Philip that he be baptized immediately. The account of this event then specifically states that Philip and the Ethiopian "went down into the water" (Acts 8:38, NKJV).

> (You were) buried with Him in baptism, in which you also were raised with Him through faith in the working of God, who raised Him from the dead.
>
> Colossians 2:12 (NKJV)

Nowhere does Jesus or any of the New Testament writers explicitly order new believers to be baptized by immersion. However, the Scriptures do strongly imply through the account of the Ethiopian's baptism that the acceptable mode of baptism during the New Testament era was immersion, because the account of this baptism shows us clearly that: (1) The Ethiopian was not baptized until after he had accepted Christ as his Savior, (2) the Ethiopian and Philip both "went down into the water," and (3) the Ethiopian and Philip both "came up out of the water" (Acts 8:39, NKJV). By entering a nearby body of water and being immersed in that water, the Ethiopian official was showing his personal identification with the death, burial, and resurrection of Jesus.

Who should be baptized?

Now that you know more about baptism from the perspective of Scripture, it should be easier to understand why baptism is not appropriate for infants and small children. Instead, this ordinance of the church is designed for adults and for children who are mature enough to understand that salvation is the necessary prerequisite for baptism. Children can certainly be baptized, because children can certainly make a personal decision to invite Christ into their hearts. But a child must choose to be baptized because that child has been saved, not because the child is following the example or the wishes of his or her parents.

> You can be baptized more than one time. Your parents may have had you baptized when you were a child, but now as an adult you are confirming the act that your parents performed. Getting baptized again adds to the work that they started.

So it is clear that water baptism is for new believers who want to openly proclaim their decision to follow Christ. But "re-baptism" can also be appropriate for the individual who was baptized earlier in his or her life, yet who never had a real salvation experience or fell away from the Lord and has since made a recommitment to Christ.

If that's you, and you are a new Christian or a person who desires to be baptized a second time because of a genuine salvation experience or a sincere rededication to Christ, please sign up on our church's website for our next baptismal service. At Creative Church, we baptize people once every month. We would love to have you participate in this powerful and meaningful expression of your newfound faith in Christ.

Questions for thought and discussion

1. According to Pastor Jonathan, water baptism is an outward expression of an inward _____ (fill in the blank). In your opinion, why would water baptism be meaningless for the person who has not been saved? Could there be any negative consequences to being baptized without being saved?

_____

_____

_____

_____

2. Baptism is also the public profession of an individual's faith and salvation. In your opinion, why would God want us to participate in an ordinance that is designed to be a public display of our individual experiences with him?

_____

_____

_____

_____

3. How is water baptism an act of worship?

_____

_____

_____

_____

4. Were you baptized when you were a child or before you were truly saved? If so, how did that experience affect you? Now that you are saved, do you believe it would be a good idea to be re-baptized? Why?

_____

_____

_____

_____

Chapter 4

The Holy Spirit
Isn't Weird

The Holy Spirit isn't "the force" that empowered Luke Skywalker. The Holy Spirit isn't a principle that binds things together. The Holy Spirit isn't the universe or the rocks or the rivers or the oceans or life itself. The Holy Spirit is a person. He is a part of the triune (three in one) Godhead.

You see, God isn't like you and me. He isn't a glorified human being. All you have to do is to take a long, hard look at the vastness of God's creation, and you will quickly understand that the Creator who made all of that is far above anything or anyone that we know in this present world.

In fact, if you really want to stretch your mental capabilities to the breaking point, try wrapping your brain around these three facts from the Bible:

- FACT #1: God is three persons (Father, Son, and Holy Spirit).
- FACT #2: Each person is fully God.

- FACT #3: There is only one God.

In other words, the God who is revealed in the Bible is one entity, yet three distinct persons, and that is why we refer to God as a Trinity. The Holy Spirit is one of these three persons and is therefore equal in power and authority to the Father and the Son. The Holy Spirit is God, so he shares all the attributes (traits and qualities) of God.

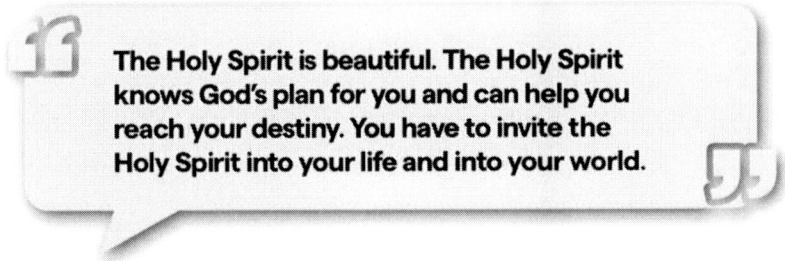

> **The Holy Spirit is beautiful. The Holy Spirit knows God's plan for you and can help you reach your destiny. You have to invite the Holy Spirit into your life and into your world.**

There is no perfect illustration of the Trinity in the world that we know. No human has ever encountered a living creature that is three distinct beings yet one being at the same time. God is unfathomable and beyond our knowing, but perhaps one illustration that could help us partially understand the nature of the Trinity is the illustration of water.

Water can be experienced in three different forms. At normal temperatures, water is a liquid that we refer to affectionately as H_2O. But if the temperature gets really cold, that H_2O will become ice, a solid substance. And if the temperature gets really hot, that same H_2O will become steam, which is a gas. Yet all three forms are the same chemical composition, H_2O (two atoms of hydrogen and one atom of oxygen). Of course, this illustration isn't perfect, because H_2O cannot be solid, liquid, and gaseous at the same time. Nevertheless, the illustration can help your mind start its journey toward grasping the fact that God isn't like you or me: He is unique in all the universe. He made us; we didn't make him.

But while the three persons of the Trinity are presented as being equal in power and authority and described as sharing the same attributes, they are also represented as being focused upon distinct roles in their relationship to mankind. The Father, for instance, is always associated with creation. The Son (Jesus) is always associated with redemption. The Holy Spirit is associated with the work of regeneration in the believer's life.

> In Him you also trusted, after you heard the word of truth, the gospel of your salvation; in whom also, having believed, you were sealed with the Holy Spirit of promise, who is the guarantee of our inheritance until the redemption of the purchased possession, to the praise of His glory.
>
> **Ephesians 1:13-14 (NKJV)**

A bad rap

Some people believe that the Holy Spirit is weird, because a lot of undisciplined and ill-informed people have done a lot of strange things in the name of the Holy Spirit. But this "weirdness" is the fault of the people who engage in it, not the fault of the Spirit himself. Different people simply respond to the Holy Spirit's presence in different ways, and some of them have never been taught the appropriate, biblical way to react to a move of God's Spirit. That's why the Holy Spirit often gets the "credit" for a lot of bizarre behaviors that are the result of merely human activity.

No, the Holy Spirit isn't weird. People can be weird sometimes, but the Holy Spirit is beautiful, and he is powerful in the believer's life. There is nothing weird about watching the Holy Spirit set a person free from a lifelong addiction. There is nothing weird about watching the Holy Spirit heal and restore a broken marriage. There is nothing weird about watching the Holy Spirit take a broken person and fill that person's soul with joy, peace, love, hope, or contentment.

> **People worship differently. At Creative Church we make the worship experience meaningful without introducing practices that might take the focus away from Jesus.**

The Holy Spirit is not weird at all. In fact, one of the symbols used in the Bible to depict the Holy Spirit is the symbol of a dove, and a dove isn't weird in any way. A dove is gentle, and a dove invokes a sense of peace. If I had a dove on my shoulder and I started doing weird and bizarre things, that dove would fly away. But I don't want the Holy Spirit to "fly away" from me. I want the Holy Spirit to be with me in order to empower me as I minister on the Lord's behalf. Therefore, I will respect the Holy Spirit and avoid any tendency to "act out" in a strange way while I am representing him to other people. I will also allow the Holy Spirit to "check" me when I feel like verbalizing some of the outlandish things that pop into my head. I would encourage you to do the same. Learn to listen to the Holy Spirit when he says, "Don't do that!"

> **Do you not know that you are the temple of God and that the Spirit of God dwells in you?**
> I Corinthians 3:16 (NKJV)

However, don't misunderstand my appeal for order and decency. At Creative Church, we do believe in the gifts of the Spirit, and we do give opportunity for those gifts to be manifested in our services. We simply choose to enjoy the manifestations of the Spirit at the proper time and to do so with decency and with order.

For instance, nobody in our church should be offended whenever we gather for the purpose of allowing the Holy Spirit to manifest his presence in our lives, because nobody in our church will ever be forced to attend one of these services. In addition, whenever we assemble for the purpose of making ourselves available to the Holy Spirit, we will always follow the advice of the apostle Paul by exercising the gifts of the Spirit in proper ways. We won't allow misguided or misinformed people to usurp the "flow" of the Holy Spirit.

As you start attending Creative Church, you will soon notice that Sundays aren't designed for visible or audible manifestations of the Holy Spirit, because Sundays are devoted to winning lost souls. Jesus promised his disciples that he would make them "fishers of men" (Matthew 4:19, NKJV). So on Sundays, we "fish." We preach the simple message of salvation, and we invite unbelievers to come to Christ. But on other occasions, we set aside special times, not to "fish," but rather to "swim" in the presence of the Holy Spirit, and those are the times when we allow the Spirit of God to minister to us through prophecies, healings, miracles, words of knowledge, words of wisdom, and all the other spiritual manifestations that are enumerated and explained in the New Testament.

> **During worship God washes our hearts, and He heals us. That is why someone might start tearing up next to you. They are being touched by God.**

So we "swim" at appropriate times and in appropriate settings, but we devote Sundays to "fishing." And we never mix these two distinct styles of worship, because, as Paul so eloquently explained in I Corinthians 14, when you fish where you swim, you end up scaring away the fish. "To everything there is a season, a time for every purpose under heaven" (Ecclesiastes 3:1, NKJV).

What is praying in tongues?

Tongues are real, and they are biblical. The apostle Paul prayed in tongues (see I Corinthians 14:18), and Paul taught other believers to pray in tongues (see I Corinthians 14:39). In addition, there is absolutely nothing in the Bible that teaches us that the gift of tongues is no longer relevant for modern believers. If the power of the Holy Spirit was necessary for success in the Christian life during the 1st century, the power of the Holy Spirit is relevant for success in the Christian life today. God wants you to be open to the Holy Spirit as you grow in your knowledge of him and your personal experience with him.

> **If you love Me, keep My commandments. And I will pray the Father, and He will give you another Helper, that He may abide with your forever—the Spirit of truth, whom the world cannot receive.**
>
> John 14:15-17 (NKJV)

Like the other manifestations of the Holy Spirit, the gift of tongues is not weird if it is utilized in the way God intended and for the purpose God intended. Tongues is something the Holy Spirit teaches us to do so we can pray the way we need to pray about things we cannot fully understand.

Most of the things we pray about are things that are clear-cut, things that can be rationally understood. For example, if a person is praying about a decision he must make between accepting a new job opportunity or staying at his current job, that decision will most likely boil down to some very practical considerations like the family's finances, the family's lifestyle, and the feelings that the person has about the work he is currently doing and the environment in which he is doing it. There's usually nothing mysterious about the prayers we pray when we are faced with everyday challenges and decisions. However, when a person encounters a problem, a challenge, or an opportunity that presents itself as a total enigma, that person will need the Holy Spirit's guidance and personal intervention in order to know what he should do. In fact, he will need divine guidance just to know how he should pray in those situations.

The apostle Paul told us that "we do not know what we should pray for as we ought" (Romans 8:26, NKJV). But in that same verse, Paul went on to tell us that, when times like this come and we need to better understand how God wants us to pray, "the Spirit also helps in our weaknesses." In fact, the Spirit of God "makes intercession for us with groanings which cannot be uttered." So when a person wants God's perfect will for his or her life and that person isn't sure what God's will might be, it is reassuring to know that the Holy Spirit is capable of praying through us.

Sometimes, however, these kinds of prayers can't be expressed in everyday speech. Sometimes, they become cries of the heart that "cannot be uttered." In other words, prayers like this sometimes become expressions that bear no resemblance at all to human language. So never forget: Prayer "in the Holy Spirit" is always acceptable when you are alone with God in your "cool place," because praying in tongues can never frighten away any fish when God is the only one listening. To the contrary, praying in tongues in the privacy of your private place of prayer can allow you to communicate with God on a level that is impossible with strictly human words.

> One of the Bible's words for the Holy Spirit is paraclete, which means "one who stands beside you and enables you to continue on your spiritual walk."

The paraclete

If you want a perfectly accurate depiction of the Holy Spirit, pay attention to the way Jesus introduced him to the apostles. Jesus told his disciples that he was going to pray for them. He was going to ask the Father to give them "another Helper (in my place), that He may abide with you forever—the Spirit of truth, whom the world cannot receive… (John 14:15-17, NKJV). The word that Jesus used in this sentence for "Helper" is the Greek word *paraclete*, which means "someone who stands alongside you." In other words, Jesus was going to ask the Father to send the Holy Spirit to stand alongside these men in Jesus' place after he had ascended into Heaven.

> **But the fruit of the Spirit is love, joy, peace, longsuffering, kindness, goodness, faithfulness, gentleness, self-control.**
> **Galatians 5:22-23 (NKJV)**

Jesus wanted his disciples to know that he would never leave them. His presence would be with them—in the form of the Holy Spirit—wherever they went to build the kingdom of God. The Holy Spirit, therefore, was sent to stand alongside you:

- To help guide you in your Christian walk
- To help reveal God's will and purposes to you
- To help strengthen you with boldness as you face a spiritually hostile world
- To help comfort you when you mourn
- To help teach you how to pray when you aren't sure how to pray
- To help you better understand God, yourself, and others
- To help you succeed in the Christian life by endowing you with spiritual gifts
- To help build Christian character within you

This is what the Holy Spirit was sent to do in our lives. This is what the Holy Spirit was sent to do in our homes and our churches. So we need to practice our response to him and our response to his presence in our lives. At home, we need to practice how we respond to the Holy Spirit's presence so we will know how to respond to him in church. And in church, we need to practice how we respond to the Holy Spirit's presence so we will know how to respond to him in our homes and on our jobs and everywhere else that we interact with people, because the Holy Spirit is God's gift to the church, and the church is God's gift to humanity. But the church only has power and influence when it is anointed and emboldened by the presence and the power of the Holy Spirit.

The Holy Spirit isn't weird; the Holy Spirit is beautiful. But we will never learn to appreciate the full blessings of his beauty if we don't learn to appreciate and celebrate his presence in our lives and our churches. Invite the Holy Spirit to become the dominant influence in your life.

Questions for thought and discussion

1. Before you were saved, what came into your mind when you heard a minister or any other believer talk about the Holy Spirit?

_____

_____

_____

_____

2. Can you recall the first time you attended a gathering of Christians who were manifesting the gifts of the Holy Spirit? What were your impressions of that experience? What conclusions did you draw about the Holy Spirit and about Christianity as a whole? How do you view that experience now?

_____

_____

_____

_____

3. The apostle Paul told the first-century believers in Rome that the Holy Spirit "makes intercession for us with groanings which cannot be uttered" (Romans 8:26, NKJV). How could it benefit your prayer

life if you learned to let the Holy Spirit pray through you when appropriate?

----

4. According to Pastor Jonathan, the Holy Spirit is our Helper (paraclete). Can you give some examples of ways that the Holy Spirit has helped you during the initial days of your Christian experience?

Chapter 5

Creative Church

The church is God's gift to the world. So the things we do in church aren't man's ideas; they are God's ideas. However, the church is filled with human beings—imperfect, flawed, fragile, and wounded human beings. And for this reason, a church—even though it is a place where God dwells—can be imperfect, and it can offer up a lot of opportunities for conflict.

As you begin your Christian journey and as you start studying the Word of God, you will quickly realize that most of the books of the New Testament are letters that were written by the apostle Paul and by other early church leaders to the newly established churches throughout the Mediterranean world. You will also come to realize that the vast majority of these letters were written to help these churches deal with problems within their own church families.

At Creative Church, we exist to serve people. On God's behalf and in his name, we reach out to lost and broken souls to help them find salvation through Christ and to help them rise to their full potentials in the Lord. But because we are trying to be creative (moving beyond traditional methods of ministry) and because we deal with flawed and broken human beings, we also have our challenges and we sometimes make mistakes. That is why a clear understanding of what the church is designed to be is invaluable to you as you seek to find your rightful place in the family of God, because it is inevitable: You *will* get hurt by your church and your church family. The development of meaningful relationships where accountability, intimacy, and honesty are foundational is a journey that is fraught with peril.

> **For where two or three are gathered together in My name, I am there in the midst of them.**
>
> **Matthew 18:20 (NKJV)**

A hospital, not a courtroom

For starters, Creative Church is a hospital, not a courtroom. We exist to heal and restore people in the name of Christ, not to judge people or condemn them. For this reason, we give people room to be human. We give them room to make mistakes, because it's okay to make a mistake, but not to be a mistake.

Our driving motivation as a body of Jesus' followers is to help each person who enters our doors discover the Lord and find a sense of belonging in a spiritual family of like-minded believers. We also want to help each person learn to serve the Lord in creative ways so that that person will have the courage to be a living witness for Christ by learning to "own" his or her own story. But if we sincerely believe that we exist to be a spiritual hospital—a place where people can be forgiven, healed, delivered, and restored—we can't create an invisible list of sicknesses that we refuse to treat. Rather, we must be willing to accept all people, regardless of a person's problems or past failures. We must be willing to open our arms to all people just as they are when they drive onto our campus, and we must be willing to meet them and help them where they are. That's what Jesus did. Can we do less as we minister in his name?

> **The church is God's idea, not man's idea. Jesus died for the church, His bride.**

Beyond healing

Like any hospital, however, Creative Church doesn't want its "patients" to stay sick. Eventually, we hope to see the people who attend our church gain victory over their pasts and move forward into God's perfect will for their lives. We expect them to give up their beds so that new "patients" can take their places.

That's where ministry and service enter into the picture as part of the process of spiritual growth. Although you were once part of God's problem, the Holy Spirit wants to help you become part of God's solution for other people. He wants to take your previous wounds and use the wisdom and experience you derived from those wounds in order to help others grow and succeed.

Church life must be a lot more than just an hour or so of celebration each week. It's important to celebrate God's presence and to bask in the joy of the Holy Spirit when we gather. But the Christian life, just like life in the physical world, is a balance of competing experiences and obligations. Consequently, when God saved you and adopted you into his family, he didn't intend for you to live perpetually as a beneficiary of other people's ministries. Instead, God wants you to "grow up" spiritually and to become someone who ministers to others in his name.

Hospitals are not filled with healthy people; they are filled with people who want to be healthy. Hospitals are not filled with healthy people; they are filled with talented workers who are there to serve the sick folks who come to them for help. In fact, the typical American hospital has about 16 workers for every available bed, because it takes a lot of workers and a lot of different skills to help broken people become whole.

That's why, at Creative Church, we encourage all members of our church family to roll up their sleeves and to get involved serving others. And you don't have to wait until you attain a certain level of spiritual perfection to get involved, because the day of your perfection will never arrive while you remain in your mortal body. But by getting busy and getting involved, you can actually accelerate your own spiritual growth while helping others become healthier, as well.

As the pastor of Creative Church, I enjoy the benefit of having a clearly defined job description. My job description was written by the apostle Paul, and it can be found in Ephesians 4:11-13. Paul, writing to the church in Ephesus, said, "(The Lord) Himself gave some to be... pastors." Why? "For the equipping of the saints for the work of the ministry." Notice that Paul didn't say it was the pastor's job to do the work of the ministry in the church. Paul said it was the pastor's job to equip, to train, and to prepare all the people in the church to do the necessary works of service.

God has given gifts, talents, and abilities to everyone, and a lot of those special gifts are listed in the Bible. They range from teaching to serving and from hospitality to encouraging. Your job is to make yourself available to help meet one or more of these needs within the church; my job is to give you the training, the tools, and the authority that you need to do it. But regardless of what you choose to do, God wants you to use your gifts and talents to serve other people in his name. He wants you to use your gifts and talents to make him famous, not yourself.

Some people believe that work is a curse on humanity, but work wasn't part of God's curse on fallen humanity. Instead, from the very beginning, work was a blessing. God created Adam and gave him a job before sin entered the picture and before God ever cursed the ground. Likewise, work will be a part of life in Heaven. We aren't going to Heaven to float around on clouds and play harps. We are going there to worship and to serve the Lord. Church is simply a practice run for Heaven. It's a warm-up session for all that awaits us. Solomon wrote, "Whatever your hands find to do, do it with your might" (Ecclesiastes 9:10, NKJV). Do it with excellence, and do it as unto the Lord, because, if you do, he will reward you in this life and throughout eternity.

Service to the Lord will also accelerate your Christian growth. Jesus didn't die for you so you could do nothing; he died for you so you could do something that will have eternal value in his eyes. And surprisingly, it is always the "little" things, the less spectacular things that capture God's attention and command his satisfaction with us. He told his followers that they would be rewarded for simply offering a cup of cold water in his name (see Matthew 10:42).

> **For as we have many members in one body, but all the members do not have the same function, so we, being many, are one body in Christ, and individually members of one another.**
>
> Romans 12:4-5 (NKJV)

Beyond isolation

Involvement is an important element in your Christian growth, but relationship is the other column upon which the church stands. God looks upon his people as a family, not as a large group of rugged, self-sufficient individuals. He wants us to interact in order to become part of each other's lives so we can encourage one another, instruct one another, support one another, pray for one another, and hold one another accountable.

But to create a true spiritual family, the members of Creative Church must always remember that the people who come here aren't perfect. They aren't always healthy. These people are seeking health and they are working toward better spiritual health, but they have not yet attained anything approaching spiritual maturity, so we must interact with them in grace. We must be willing to accept them with their faults and stick by their sides as they work to overcome their weaknesses.

Remember, hospitals aren't filled with healthy people; they are filled with sick people who want to become healthy. So don't be surprised if somebody in the church lies to you or steals from you or rejects you or offends you in some way. This doesn't mean that the hospital itself is unhealthy; it simply means that there are a lot of "patients" in the hospital who still need help in achieving spiritual perfection.

> **We are instructed to love and forgive one another and to share the love of God with those who are still lost.**

Paul told the believers at the church in Philippi to "forbear" one another in love (see Ephesians 4:2, KJV). That's a very interesting word choice. In today's terminology, that means to "put up with" one another or to "tolerate" one another. In a church setting, we have to learn not to expect super-human things from mere mortal human beings. We have to learn not to expect too much from people who are "being transformed" into the image of Christ (II Corinthians 3:18, NKJV). In other words, they're not there yet.

Sometimes you may hurt or disappoint others, and sometimes others may hurt or disappoint you. But God hasn't placed you in an environment where everybody will love you and treat you with respect all the time; he has placed you in an environment where you can love everybody else and treat them with respect. And fortunately, God has given you a lot of guidance on how to develop these kinds of healthy relationships within the body of Christ and how to heal those relationships that are broken. He has given you clear-cut instruction regarding forgiveness and reconciliation.

Life's most meaningful and enduring relationships aren't created in a pristine environment, and they aren't forged in naiveté. Rather, the strongest relationships are always built in three stages:

- Stage 1 – you're in each other's eyes
  You watch one another and size one another up. You study one another's mannerisms and examine one another's ways in order to determine whether you want to pursue a mutual relationship. And sometimes you do this subconsciously.

> And He Himself gave some to be apostles, some prophets, some evangelists, and some pastors and teachers, for the equipping of the saints for the work of ministry, for the edifying of the body of Christ, till we all come to the unity of the faith and of the knowledge of the Son of God, to a perfect man, to the measure of the stature of the fullness of Christ....
>
> Ephesians 4:11-13 (NKJV)

- Stage 2 – you're in each other's way
  Once you get a little comfortable with each other, you start testing the limitations of your evolving relationship. You start saying things you would never say to a complete stranger. You start questioning one another, advising one another, and cautiously intruding into one another's personal affairs. And while these intrusions may create some conflict, they also become the foundation of an enduring relationship, because, with each "test," the other person either chooses to close the door on the relationship or to respond by opening his own heart and mind more completely to you.
- Stage 3 – you're in each other's heart
  Once you reach this stage, you will have a sizeable backlog of wounds and offenses, but those things won't matter, because the joy and the richness provided by a true, meaningful relationship will be worth the emotional price you had to pay in order to achieve it.

Conclusion

God saves us so he can perfect us, he heals us so he can use us for his glory, and the church is the place where God achieves his goal of perfecting his image in us. But the church is more than just a place to sing and to listen to Bible-based teaching. The church is a place where people come to find forgiveness for the past and purpose for the future. It is a place where they come to find freedom from those things that have brought them pain in life and a place where they can belong. This is why it is important to be "planted" in a church, not to float in and out of one or to wander from one church to another. As the psalmist declared, "Those who are planted in the house of the Lord shall flourish in the courts of our God" (Psalm 92:13, NKJV). If you want to grow up to be strong and healthy (spiritually speaking), you need to have a church home.

> ## Creativity takes courage.

But while the truths that are proclaimed at church can set people free, grace makes it possible for a church to function as a true spiritual family, especially in an environment where new and creative models of ministry are attracting people from all walks of life and from all imaginable backgrounds.

So we invite you to get involved. We invite you to make yourself available for acts of service. We also invite you to start doing the hard work of building relationships with people who can help you grow as a Christian. Start attending a small group and start serving in one of our entry-level ministries, whether your service is once a week, once a month, or once a year.

When Jesus was in Cana in Galilee, he turned water into wine. But the water only became wine after it was poured out of the jars. What you might regard as simple "water" in your life may actually be a gift that God wants you to share with other people, because, once you pour yourself out for the Lord, your simple offering of "water" can become a gift of full-bodied wine. It can nourish and enrich all who are refreshed by it.

Questions for thought and discussion

1. In Chapter 5, Pastor Jonathan wrote, "Creative Church is a
_____ (fill in the blank), not a courtroom." What does that

mean to you? How can the church denounce sin while granting grace to people who do sinful things?

_____

_____

_____

_____

2. Fill in the blanks in this statement from Chapter 5: "Although you were once part of God's _____, the Holy Spirit wants to help you become part of God's _____ for other people." Explain!

_____

_____

_____

3. God has given gifts, talents, and abilities to everyone. List one or two "gifts" that God has given to you. How might God use your gifts to advance the work of his kingdom?

_____

_____

_____

_____

4. Comparing the church to a hospital, Pastor Jonathan wrote that "hospitals aren't filled with healthy people; they are filled with sick people who want to become healthy." What "sickness" did you bring with you when you first started attending Creative Church? How did God use the church to heal you?

_____

_____

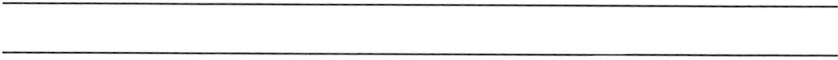

Chapter 6

Telling Your Story

Shortly before he ascended into Heaven, Jesus told his disciples something very important. He said, "But you shall receive power when the Holy Spirit has come upon you; and you shall be witnesses to Me in Jerusalem, and in all Judea and Samaria, and to the end of the earth." (Acts 1:8, NKJV). In other words, Jesus wanted his followers to tell the world about his love and his power to save people from the emptiness of a meaningless life. But how can an average person, untrained in the finer points of theology, "bear witness" to someone as glorious and profound as Jesus? The best way, by far, to point people toward Jesus is to simply tell them the story about your own life and what Jesus has done for you.

Your testimony (personal story) is your greatest witnessing tool. Being willing to talk to other people about the things God has done for you is the key to sharing your faith in the most powerful and profound way. You see, people aren't interested in your knowledge of the Bible, so you don't need to be a scholar to tell them about the Lord. People are only interested in your testimony, the honest story of the real things God has done for you. Nothing could possibly impact people more than that, and they will know, when you share it, that your story is true and your experience real.

Of course, it takes a certain amount of courage to approach a person about something as private as that person's faith. But by simply looking for appropriate opportunities to tell your own story, you can break through the walls that people erect in order to hide their secrets and their wounds. The ups and downs that you have experienced in life can become the key that God uses to unlock another person's destiny.

> **Ask God daily who He wants you to share your story with. Boldly share what God has done for you. What may seem like a simple truth to you can be exactly what that person needs to hear.**

No regrets

There's a statement we often use around Creative Church that will directly apply to your ability to witness for Christ. Around Creative Church, we often say, "'Oh well' is better than 'what if.'" And we often repeat that statement because it perfectly summarizes the way a believer should think about his or her willingness to talk to other people about the Lord.

We especially repeat this statement around our church's teenagers, because we want to encourage our young people to be bold in their efforts to share their faith with other teens. Statistics tell us that about 65 percent of all communications between teenagers are conducted through a screen (a computer, laptop, or cellphone). So teens, who are persistent and technologically advanced in their communications practices, have a wonderful opportunity to touch and impact other teenagers with their individual stories. That is important, considering the extreme social pressures that are placed upon young people today and the high risk of suicide that accompanies it.

In our home state of Minnesota, for instance, approximately 1,000 teenagers take their own lives each year, and that is due to the mounting social pressures that are placed upon teens, who lack the experience and maturity to cope with such pressures. Since suicide is the third leading cause of death among teenagers in Minnesota and since teens communicate with one another prolifically through technology, we want the young people at our church to understand the necessity of sharing their faith with their friends. We want them to understand that "oh well" is a whole lot better than "what if."

> But you shall receive power when the Holy Spirit has come upon you; and you shall be witnesses to Me in Jerusalem, and in all Judea and Samaria, and to the end of the earth.
> **Acts 1:8 (NKJV)**

In other words, we explain to our teenagers that it is much better to say, "Oh well, I did my best to engage that person," or "Oh well, I tried to tell them about Jesus, but they just blew me off," or "Oh well, I told that person my story, but she just acted like she wasn't interested" than it is to say, "What if I had said something before my friend took his own life" or "What if I had just mustered enough courage to save that kid's life."

The same principle applies to adults. Would you rather say to yourself, "Oh well, I did my best to tell my friend (relative, coworker, etc.) how God turned my life around," or would you prefer to say, "What if I had been courageous enough to say something before his marriage fell apart" or "What if I had spoken up before she passed into eternity without knowing God's forgiveness?" There is no better and simpler way to put it: It is better to go through life enduring a whole lot of "oh well's" than it is to face even a few of those painful "what if's."

Remember, you don't have to be a theologian to tell people about Jesus, and you don't have to be a good debater either. Effective witnessing is not the result of carefully rehearsed talking points or the ability to "sell" yourself or the Lord. Effective witnessing is the result of simply telling people your own true story. Nothing will ever impact a person more than that. In fact, the thing that impressed people the most about the disciples was not their knowledge of the Scriptures; it was the fact that they had been changed because they had been with Jesus (see Acts 4:13). An honest testimony is an anointed testimony, and the Holy Spirit will use your honest testimony to touch and convict people's hearts.

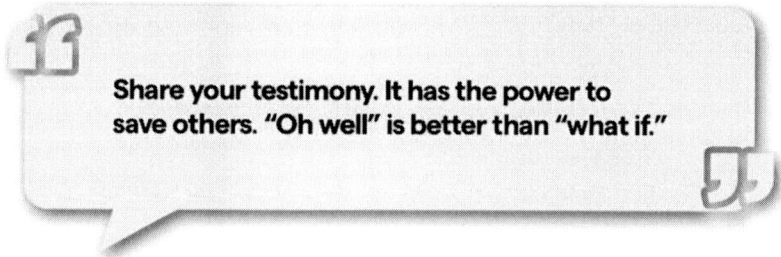

> Share your testimony. It has the power to save others. "Oh well" is better than "what if."

Your beautiful, beautiful scars

Many years ago, God taught me something that has radically changed the way I approach my ministry. God taught me that when he heals us, he always leaves his "medicine" inside us so we can share it with other people. This means that God will heal our wounds, but he won't always heal our scars. He wants to use our scars to convince others of the healing power that is available to them.

Jesus himself is the best example of this principle. When Jesus was crucified, his body was terribly abused, and perhaps the worst of his wounds were the wounds to his hands and his side. Jesus' body was affixed to the cross when the Roman executioners drove nails through his hands, and Jesus died shortly before a Roman soldier thrust a spear into his side. But while God healed Jesus' wounds, raising him from the dead, the scars on his hands and his side were never healed. In fact, those scars became the proof of his death and resurrection. When Thomas, one of Jesus' disciples, refused to believe the reports that Jesus had risen from the dead, Jesus appeared to Thomas and allowed Thomas to look at his scars and touch them so that Thomas would know that this was truly Jesus.

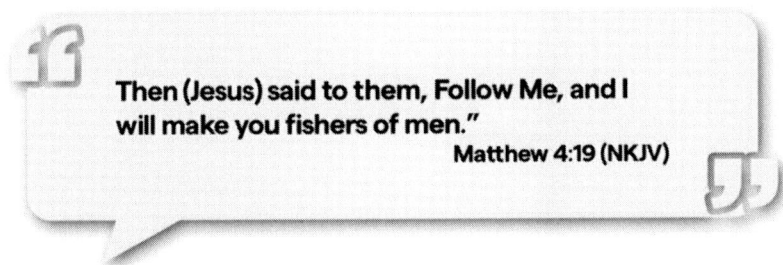

> Then (Jesus) said to them, Follow Me, and I will make you fishers of men."
> Matthew 4:19 (NKJV)

When we get saved, we usually want God to heal our scars, because we don't want people to see the consequences of our past mistakes and failures. We don't want people to see the evidence of what we've endured in life. In fact, society and human nature both teach us that we should hide our scars to conceal them from human observation. We should cover our physical scars with makeup, clothing, or a carefully crafted haircut. And we should cover our invisible scars by remaining silent about them in our interactions with others.

But God doesn't heal our scars. In the same way that he raised Jesus from the dead yet refused to heal Jesus' scars, God will transform our lives and heal our inner wounds, but he will seldom remove the scars that we bear as a consequence of our former lives. Instead, he leaves those scars, because our scars are meant to serve as a constant reminder to ourselves and to others of what God is able to do. They remind us of God's power to change, to heal, and to deliver. The prophet Isaiah, speaking about Jesus, wrote, "But he was wounded for our transgressions, He was bruised for our iniquities; the chastisement for our peace was upon Him, and by His stripes we are healed" (Isaiah 53:5, NKJV).

But until you show somebody your scars, you won't be able to fully understand why God doesn't want you to hide them, and until you show a person your scars, that person won't be able to fully understand what it means to follow Christ. Without a doubt, your scars are your greatest witnessing tools because they can speak more loudly and more eloquently than any words you could utter. They can testify convincingly of God's love and his power to forgive, to save, and to change a person's life.

> **When God heals you, He leaves the medicine inside you so you can help others find peace, joy, and purpose.**

Our scars say to other people, "If God got me through this, then he can get you through your problems, too." So by sharing your story and by showing your scars to others in honest and transparent ways, you can turn your misery into a source of ministry and your pain into a source of praise. You can touch and heal a person's soul and help that person find a new life and eternal hope in Jesus… something that could never be achieved through a cleverly crafted theological argument.

The role of passion

A person with an experience is never at the mercy of a person with an opinion, so the passion that you have about your own personal experience with Christ will be the most powerful and convincing asset you could ever have in your service to God. Unfortunately, familiarity can sometimes stifle passion, and that is a reality you must always guard against.

Let me explain it this way: When you first got engaged, you were probably so passionate about your approaching wedding, everybody could see your obvious joy. When you first got saved, the same kind of passion was undoubtedly evident to the people who knew you best. Your responsibility going forward is to retain that passion by developing a habit of telling your story to others and explaining to them how God healed your wounds. Believe me, there is no "high" in the Christian life quite like the "high" you will experience when you lead another soul to Christ. So soul-winning is contagious. Once you start doing it, your passion will never subside.

> **And daily in the temple, and in every house, they did not cease teaching and preaching Jesus as the Christ.**
>
> **Acts 5:42 (NKJV)**

Several years ago, when I was boarding an airplane for the first leg of a long flight, a young lady sat in the seat beside me, and I could tell almost instantly that this young lady wanted to talk to me. I don't usually strike up conversations with strangers, especially when I travel, so I followed my normal routine of putting headphones over my ears, pulling a hoodie over my head, and putting sunglasses over my eyes so I could avoid the potential of any human interaction that might lure me into a boring conversation.

But in spite of all my efforts to appear unapproachable, it was obvious to me that this young woman, probably in her mid-20s, still wanted to talk. So once we reached cruising altitude, she finally worked up the courage to tap me on my shoulder. At that point, there was nothing more I could do to avoid a conversation with her.

"Can I help you?" I asked.

"Sir, I'm sorry to bother you," she replied. "But I just have to ask you, do you know Jesus?" Wearing one of the most dazzling and amazing smiles I have ever seen, she wanted to know if I was saved and destined for Heaven.

So I told her, "Well, yes, I do know Jesus. In fact, I'm a pastor." And we talked about the Lord for the duration of our flight.

> **Jesus came to His own, and they rejected Him, denied Him, and crucified Him.**
> **Hebrews 12 reminds us that mere rejection should never stop us from sharing the gospel with others.**

Once we landed and had exited the plane, we had a final opportunity to encourage one another and to actually pray for one another right there in the airport. Then we went our separate ways as I took the long walk through the terminal to the gate for my connecting flight. But as I approached the gate, pulling my carry-on behind me, the Holy Spirit spoke to me in an unmistakable way, convicting me on the spot and forcing me to confront the fact that I had lost my passion for witnessing.

When that realization struck me, I actually stood there and wept in the airport as the Holy Spirit spoke gently, yet firmly to my heart, conveying the truth to me that "Jonathan, you had no intentions of asking that young lady the question that she eventually asked you. You had no intentions of asking her if she knew Jesus."

What has happened to me? I wondered to myself. *I'm a pastor. I'm a ministry leader. I teach others the importance of sharing Christ, yet I have become stale and indifferent, and I have lost my passion for telling people about the Lord.* And ever since that day, when God used a courageous young woman to teach me a valuable lesson, I have always tried to make it my highest priority to share Christ with others. I have always tried to find appropriate ways to ask the people that I meet, "Do you know Jesus?"

Conclusion.

You can't have a testimony without a test. By exhibiting the courage to share your story with another, you will keep the bright light of your spiritual passion burning for as long as you put yourself in the position of pointing people to Jesus by explaining to them what he has done for you.

> **And they overcame (the Devil) by the blood of the Lamb and by the word of their testimony.**
>
> **Revelation 12:11 (NKJV)**

That is why, at Creative Church, we often describe ourselves as a family of believers who are "showing God's love in creative ways so that people will have the courage to own their own stories." And with that stated mission in mind, I would like to encourage you to not be afraid to tell others about your own experience with the Lord. Don't be embarrassed to share your faith and the story of your changed life. Don't be hesitant, when appropriate, to share your scars in order to give people hope, because everybody you know and everybody you meet will have scars of their own that they are hiding, and they will have latent hopes and dreams that they can one day be healed of their wounds.

And once you do start sharing Jesus with other people, don't settle for being an "inviter." Be a "bringer" instead. Bring people to church with you, and walk with people until they can navigate the Christian life on their own. Research proves that 85 percent of people who are invited to church will say "yes" if you offer to personally accompany them to a church service.

Why are people willing to respond? Because people are looking for the same things you were looking for when somebody pointed you to Jesus! They are looking for hope, they are looking for significance, they are looking for healing, and they are looking for something real in their lives. Jesus is the only answer for what they are seeking.

Questions for thought and discussion

1. People at Creative Church often remind one another that "oh well" is better than "_____" (fill in the blank). In your own words, explain what this catchphrase means to you.

_____

_____

_____

_____

2. Who shared Christ with you in a way that led to your salvation? Did that person explain the gospel to you, or did that person bring you to church to hear the gospel and experience the presence of God? What lesson can you learn about witnessing from the way you discovered Christ?

_____

_____

_____

_____

3. What kind of "wounds" has God healed in your life that can equip you to share a story of deliverance and redemption with other people? What kinds of "scars" remain from that past experience?

_____

_____

_____

_____

4. Have you ever taken the bold step of sharing the gospel with an unbeliever? What happened? What is your greatest deterrent to sharing Christ with others? What can you do to overcome this limitation?

Chapter 7

We're In The
"People Business"

The first recorded words of Jesus were a question that he posed to his earthly parents, Joseph and Mary: "Did you not know that I must be about My Father's business?" (Luke 2:49, NKJV). But what was the "business" that Jesus was referring to? What was the "business" to which he would devote his entire earthly life? It was the "business" of helping people: teaching them, healing them, saving them, delivering them, equipping them, and then sending the Holy Spirit to finish the task of perfecting them.

The church, which is the body of Christ in the world, is called to carry on the work that Jesus began. We exist, therefore, to help people: to love them, to serve them, and to assist them in attaining their full potential in Christ. This means that you are the focal point of all that we do at Creative Church. But you also are part of God's solution for others who are part of this growing spiritual family.

> This is My commandment, that you love one another as I have loved you. Greater love has no one than this, than to lay down one's life for his friends.
>
> John 15:12-13 (NKJV)

Strength through diversity

Here at Creative Church, we don't have *all* things in common. We just have *one* thing in common: our love for the Lord Jesus Christ. Nothing else really matters. Jesus is our common focus and the "glue" that binds us together as a spiritual family.

Of course, this means that we are diverse in every other imaginable way. We are diverse when it comes to gender, when it comes to ethnicity, when it comes to age, education, and economic status. But these physical and financial differences don't bother us, because they are temporary, earthly distinctions. The only thing that matters for eternity will be each individual's relationship with God through Christ, so we make that point of unity our sole focus.

When it comes to our shared faith, therefore, we all believe that Jesus is the Son of God, that he died for our sins, that he was raised for our justification, and that we will dwell with him forever in Heaven. But in every other way, we are as diverse a group of people as you can find anywhere, and we have come to realize that our strength as a family of believers is found in our diversity.

Just think about it! The United States is not the most populous country in the world. Yet the United States, in virtually every one of the Olympic Games, wins more gold medals than any other country, and it does so consistently. To me, it's obvious why. It's because we have every ethnicity in the world competing together under the banner of one flag, each athlete contributing his or her own unique talents and physical abilities to the goals of the team and for the benefit of the nation they represent. China, on the other hand, although it is the most populous nation on earth, consistently lags behind the United States in overall medals, because China's population is 91.5 percent Chinese. There is little racial or ethnic diversity there.

> God loves the people that you and I have a problem with. They are His sons and daughters. We don't gather because we have all things in common. We gather because we have one thing in common—Jesus.

The apostle Paul, explaining how God intended the church to operate, wrote in one of his letters, "You are all one in Christ Jesus" (Galatians 3:28, NKJV). But Paul explained in another letter that this wonderful unity is best expressed in our amazing diversity, because, according to Paul, "There are DIFFERENT kinds of gifts, but the same Spirit that distributes them. There are DIFFERENT kinds of service, but the same Lord. There are DIFFERENT kinds of working, but in all of them in everyone it is the same God at work" (I Corinthians 12:4-6, NIV, capitalization mine).

Our diversity, therefore, is a good thing, not a bad thing. It's a God thing. But our diversity only serves its God-given purpose when it is expressed in an environment where our common devotion to Christ remains the focus of all that we do. This means that, at Creative Church, your identity is no longer found in your age, in your gender, in your ethnic heritage, or in any other worldly or earthly category. Your identity is found in the fact that God is your heavenly Father, and everybody at Creative Church shares this common heritage.

I am explaining this to you, not to negate or minimize your distinctive characteristics as a human being, but rather to put those characteristics in their proper eternal context, because, while your distinctive qualities and mine might be important in this world, they have absolutely no value in Heaven. In Heaven we will find believers from "all nations, tribes, peoples, and tongues, standing before the throne" (Revelation 7:9, NKJV).

Therefore, our first priority as a church must be to identify with Christ. Your DNA will certainly have value in the context of your earthly history and heritage, but your DNA can never determine your spiritual destiny. Your destiny will be determined by God and by your response to him.

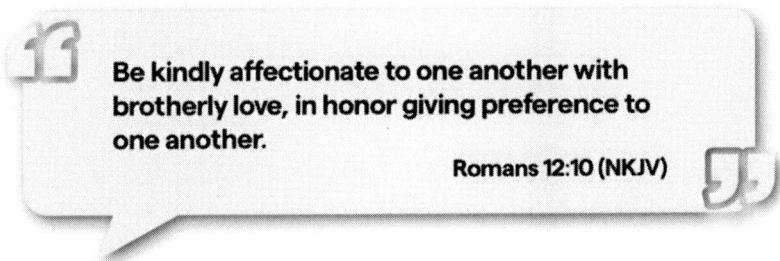

> **Be kindly affectionate to one another with brotherly love, in honor giving preference to one another.**
>
> **Romans 12:10 (NKJV)**

Refusing to take offense

At Creative Church, we believe that our diversity makes us strong. However, the fact that we are so diverse means that people from every walk of life will be entering our doors. Consequently, you need to be prepared to deal with the best that humanity has to offer, as well as the worst. And you certainly need to be prepared to be offended.

Offenses flow from our differences, but they also flow from our constant interaction with one another. When large numbers of people—people with different backgrounds and priorities, people with their own unique wounds and personal challenges—come together under one roof to share a common vision, friction can sometimes occur. So we shouldn't be surprised when someone says something or does something that others misinterpret or misunderstand.

That's why I want to encourage you at the very beginning of your Christian journey to do two things. First, I want to encourage you to work hard to avoid offending other people. Let the Holy Spirit direct your words and the attitudes that you display, especially when you may not be in agreement with the person beside you.

Second, I want to encourage you to refuse to "take up" an offense when you encounter one. Refuse to let someone else's spiritual immaturity or total disregard for your feelings affect you. Instead, learn to forgive and learn to be patient and gracious toward people as they grow in the Lord. After all, you expect God to be patient with you, so you should do the same for others. In that way, you won't give the Devil any foothold in your life or in the church, but you will give people the room they need and the acceptance they need to grow. Bitterness is a cancer. Don't let it metastasize in your soul.

> **We do for others as God has already done for us. The Lord's Prayer encourages us to ask that God forgive us our debts, sins, and transgressions as we also have forgiven others.**

Success in the Christian life isn't about finding a church where everybody is perfect; it's about finding a church where everybody is working toward perfection. And it's not about finding a church where everybody loves you; it's about finding a church where you can love everybody. If you intend to be consistent in your pursuit of the Lord, you will need to understand very quickly that, while Jesus is perfect, people aren't. People are different, and all of them have challenges, problems, and faults that can sometimes create fiction. So learn to show grace, the same kind of grace that God shows to you every day.

I have eight children, and my youngest daughter is just learning to walk. Do you think I'm going to punish my daughter whenever she stumbles or falls? No way! Do you think I'm going to reject her or withdraw from her? Absolutely not! I've already helped my other seven children learn to walk, so I know what to do. I'm going to reach down and pick her up, I'm going to help her regain her balance, I'm going to encourage her to try again, and I'm going to praise her when she succeeds.

> **For even the Son of Man did not come to be served, but to serve, and to give His life a ransom for many.**
>
> **Mark 10:45 (NKJV)**

I feel the same way toward you and every new believer who becomes part of our unique spiritual family, and I want you to feel the same way toward your "brothers" and "sisters" in Christ. I want you to give other people a reasonable amount of room to make mistakes, and I want you to refuse to "take up" an offense against them when they do. I want you to learn patience and grace, so you can help these people grow and overcome their faults.

Amazing grace

Mercy is the characteristic that God manifests when he does *not* give us what we *do* deserve; grace is the characteristic that he manifests when he *does* give us what we do *not* deserve. Therefore, because of God's grace, your life doesn't have to be defined by any one moment or any one decision that you made in the past. Instead, your life is defined by what you are destined to become when God is finished with you.

If you stop growing in your faith by allowing your past to define you, you will unintentionally do two terrible things: You will make Jesus' sacrifice for you ineffective, and you will build a permanent monument to your past failures. But it's up to you to not let that happen.

Peter and Judas were both disciples of Jesus, and, the night before Jesus was crucified, both Peter and Judas denied the Lord. Both disciples turned their back on Jesus, and both of them refused to stand with him in his darkest hour. But while Judas stopped at the point of his failure, Peter moved beyond his failure.

> **You are not a number; you're a person with a name and a story. Your story matters to us and, more importantly, it matters to God.**

Judas refused to seek or accept the Lord's forgiveness for his failure. Instead, Judas hanged himself and forever became known as the ultimate sell-out and traitor. But Peter wept and sought God's forgiveness and restoration. As a result, Peter became the most prominent leader in the early church, as well as the author of two books in the New Testament, because Peter responded to God's grace. He realized that he was a work in progress, not a perfect human being. He also realized that, in Christ, his past could not define him. His greatest days were ahead of him.

You need to see yourself the same way that Peter saw himself, and you need to see other people the exact same way. You need to see others and yourself through the eyes of God's grace. Understand where you are heading instead of where you have been. Understand where you are traveling instead of where you stand right now.

To know and to serve

As your pastor and one who will walk alongside you for the duration of your Christian journey, I want to offer you three closing words of advice that can help you sustain your enthusiasm as a believer and help you fit into this church in a way that will benefit you and everybody else who attends here.

First, I want to encourage you to engage people. In other words, make an effort to get to know the people who attend our church.

> **But he who is greatest among you shall be your servant.**
>
> Matthew 23:11 (NKJV)

Solomon, who is well known for his wisdom, wrote, "A man who has friends must himself be friendly" (Proverbs 18:24, NKJV). In other words, friendships don't just happen by accident. As you grow in the Lord, you will need strong Christian relationships in your life. But to create those relationships, you will need to do something. You will need to make an effort to meet people and to associate with them. So don't be the last to arrive and the first to leave. Engage people, and make an effort to get to know them.

Second, I want to encourage you to have a heart to serve others, in spite of their imperfections and yours.

People who fail to serve in their local church eventually end up leaving that church, because people who choose not to invest in a church will have no real ties to that church when things get hard. They will have no meaningful role in the church and no meaningful relationships. It's actually a sign of good health for the human body to extract waste (substances that are incapable of contributing to the body's operations). The Holy Spirit will also remove people from the body of Christ (the church) if those people consistently fail to contribute in any meaningful way.

Volleyball is the only sport where you will find no superstars. Why is that? Because volleyball is the only sport where the players can't claim a position, and it's the only sport where, at some point, each player must take a turn serving! Keep this analogy in mind as you ponder your role at Creative Church.

> **Love makes us give. Love is manifested in giving. God so loved that He gave. You don't love anything that you are not giving to.**

And finally, I want to encourage you to let me be part of your life. I want to volunteer to be your pastor. I want to volunteer to get to know you, to pray for you, to nourish you with the Word of God, to walk beside you during the challenging times of your life, and to help you find your rightful place in the body of Christ and in service to God. While you may have many voices speaking into your life as you grow in your knowledge of Christ—the voices of writers, the voices of online ministers, and the voices of anointed musicians— only one person can be your pastor, and I would be honored if you would allow me to fill that role in your life.

The apostle Paul reminded the believers in Corinth, "For though you might have ten thousand instructors in Christ, yet you do not have many fathers" (I Corinthians 4:15, NKJV). I want to be a spiritual "father" to you as you take your initial steps on the journey to God's perfect plan for your life. I want to teach you the things you will need to know about God and his will for your life, I want to offer you opportunities to grow in the Spirit by serving others in a meaningful way, and I want to create an environment where you can forge lifelong relationships with people who will reinforce your commitment to Christ, not sabotage it.

So welcome to Creative Church and to the imperfect, yet passionate family of Christ followers we are building here. I am glad you have found your place with us. I am glad you are on your way to the greatest life imaginable. I am glad that we will be making this glorious journey together.

Questions for thought and discussion

1. According to Pastor Jonathan, it takes two people to create a conflict: the one who offends and the one who is offended. Considering all the interactions you will have with the people at Creative Church, what steps can you take to avoid offending others? What steps can you take to avoid being offended?

----

2. Grace is at work when we get what we don't deserve from God: his blessings, his favor, his mercy, his patience. How can you reflect the grace of God in your interactions with other members of the body of Christ?

----

3. Friendships don't happen by accident. Before a friendship can be forged, two people must engage one another in some way. Rather than waiting to be engaged, what can a newcomer at Creative Church do to engage those who already attend?

----

4. It is God's plan for every believer to find meaningful ways to serve others. What gifts, talents, or abilities has God given to you

that might be beneficial to the church in its efforts to help people live successful Christian lives?

_____

_____

_____

_____

Notes

Notes

Notes

Notes

Notes

Notes